Race To The Top

Richard Riley

This book is published by   Mercian Manuals Limited
353 Kenilworth Road
Balsall Common
West Midlands
CV7 7DL.
01676 533304
www.mercianmanuals.co.uk

Distribution worldwide by the same.

ISBN 1 903088 15 1

Printed in England by Wizard Printing Services Ltd.

Contents

Acknowledgement

We are greatly indebted to the following organisation and individuals who have assisted in the production and publication of this book.

The 'Riley Motor Club' whose assistance in allowing us to use their photographic archive together with various technical and factual information has been of tremendous help.

Chris Draper (Riley Motor Club). Chris's assistance in locating a number of requirements included in the book has been a great help.

Victor Riley whose help in clarifying quite a number of historical Company facts has been invaluable to say the least.

Peter Banner whose co-operation in allowing us to use his very fine Riley Imp in the production of the dust jacket is also greatly appreciated.

Professor A.T.Birmingham who very kindly gave an overview of the book.

Whilst realising that there have been several other very fine publications published on the Riley marque, this book is in no way an attempt to challenge their authoratative knowledge.

Picture Acknowledgements

The Author wishes to offer his most sincere thanks to those individuals and organisations for supplying the photographs included in this work.

Many of Riley pictures which appear in 'Race to the Top' are the copyright of the British Motor Industry Heritage Trust and we would like to thank BMIHT for permission to use the images.

Foreword

Although 'Race To The Top' written by Richard Riley is not the first Riley book, this publication is the first personal account of one of the five Riley brothers. Richard is the son of Allan Riley, who was the second brother. This book may therefore be described as unique.

Allan's role in the family business was important, and his first key policy decision was to form the Riley Engine Company in 1903 in conjunction with Victor (my father) and Percy, the inventive genius.

However, Allan's most crucial decision was to be the launch of the Riley Motor Manufacturing Company in Aldbourne Road, Coventry in 1913, when William Riley (my grandfather), decided to cease car manufacture and allocate all his resources to the production of Riley Detachable Wire Wheels. So we have to thank Allan for ensuring the continuation of Riley car production.

After the 1914-1918 war, the Riley Motor Manufacturing Company became Midland Motor Bodies Limited, of which Allan was Managing Director. Riley car bodies were produced in this works.

I have many happy memories of Uncle Allan, who used to take me to cricket and rugby union football matches during school holidays. He enjoyed both games and had played himself in his younger days.

Victor W Riley.

I would like to dedicate this book to my wife Lynne for all her encouragement and help.

Introduction

Richard Riley's father, Allan, as you will now read was responsible for the decision to launch the Riley Motor Manufacturing Company. As time went by this Company then became Midland Motor Bodies Limited.

We hope you enjoy the history and family member's memories and also the photographs taken over the years by the family and the Riley Motor Club and others.

Richard's Recollections

My most vivid recollections of my father, Allan Riley, were at the Moor House, our home near the village of Fillongley, where I was born in 1914, the year World War I broke out. We lived in the depths of the country, six miles from Coventry.

I make no apologies for devoting much of this book to the memory of my father who, with his four brothers, gave their life's work to the development and success of the Riley organisation.

Allan Riley
1878-1963.

The Riley (family) company probably contributed more to the success of the motor car in the forty-two years of it's existence from 1896 to 1938, than most other British firms.

William Riley, my grandfather, was born in Foleshill, Coventry in 1851. In 1870 he worked alongside his father in the family weaving business which had originated in the city. His basic knowledge of engineering acquired during his apprenticeship covered the operation of weaving machinery, which stood him in good stead for the future exciting development of the motor car, although initially, he opposed such development.

In the 1880's, the prosperity of the Coventry weaving industry was in decline due to competition from Austria and Germany. He could see no future in the business, and decided to use his engineering skills in the cycle manufacturers, Bonnick & Company. In 1896 the Riley weaving business finally ceased it's activities, and in the same year the name Bonnick & Company was changed to The Riley Cycle Company Ltd. At first he was adamant that bicycles and the pony and trap were the sensible method of road transport. However, his sons Allan, Percy and Victor thought otherwise and became so enthusiastic over the early development of the motor car, that they ordered the necessary production plant with their own money plus financial help from their parents. Within two or three years, production of motor cycles and three wheelers was well under way thanks to the perseverance of the three sons.

The Tri-car, launched in 1903, regularly swept the board in competitions in the hands of Victor Riley and his brothers Allan and Stanley from 1905 onwards. My father was born in 1878, and in his early twenties, won quite a number of competition awards racing Riley motor cycles. In 1905, the 9hp Tri-car started production.

However, as early as 1898, the first four wheeled Riley car was produced as a 'one-off'. This was designed and built by Percy in the Riley Company toolroom. He started hand building the car in 1896 and it was completed in 1898. It never went into production, but was used by the Riley family for many years.

1899 Riley Royal Tricycle lovingly restored by Sqdn Ldr Harry Knight.

Victor Riley Snr & V. Leverett with 1907 Tri-car. Seen here in 1946 on the London to Brighton run enjoying themselves.

The first Riley car designed and built by Mr Percy Riley 1896-1898.

In 1903 Victor, Allan and Percy set up the Riley Engine Company in separate premises and, in due course, their father realised that their enthusiasm had not been ill placed. In 1905 they made their first production four wheeled car, the 9hp V Twin. In 1907 it was the first car in the world to be equipped with detachable wire wheels. These were of Riley's own design and manufacture, the detachable hub and spanner of which were patented by Victor and Stanley Riley in 1912. Production was rapidly increased owing to demand from other companies in Europe, and Victor Riley in conjunction with French interests, commenced the manufacture of these wheels in France. They were supplied to many French companies until the start of World War I. In 1914, Rileys were amongst the leading British motor manufacturers.

With the outbreak of World War I in August of that year, all production was subsequently turned over to the war effort until hostilities ceased in November 1918. It was agreed that no profit was to be made by the company during that period, and that after wages and salaries had been paid, the balance would be distributed to the war effort. Car production resumed in 1919. In that year Riley opened a stand at the Olympia Motorshow in London to show the new 10.8hp Riley.

The 1907 Riley 9hp V-Twin.

My earliest recollection of a motor car was when I was five years old. My father had picked me up and deposited me in the driver's seat of a Riley '10' which was produced in 1913. I grabbed the steering wheel but failed to turn it, which resulted in frustration and tears! In those days there were no such things as starter buttons. In my case maybe just as well. There were two ways to start an engine. Either coast down a hill and let in the clutch, or crank the starting handle and pull up, *never* push down, unless you wanted to break your wrist! Those early engines had a built-in backfire system. I also remember the Riley 11hp Coupé which boasted the latest fashion i.e. disc wheels. My father was of the opinion that the car was rather highly priced at around £400.

The 1910 Riley 10hp
Note the angle of the windshield. Riley were already thinking of the drag factor at this early stage!

In 1919 Victor Riley, Stanley Riley and Jesse Browning had great success in several well known trials with the Riley 10hp Speed Model. I well remember Jesse Browning who was a real character. The last time I saw him he was in his eighties and still going strong. He joined Riley as a boy starting on the factory floor. One of his jobs on the way up was as official driver to my grandfather. He prided himself on his command of the English language. He did come out with the most amazing 'long words', in fact, his colleagues accused him of swallowing a dictionary. I sometimes wondered if he knew the true meaning of every long word!!

This was now a very busy time for my father, and as a result, he had little opportunity for relaxation at home. By 1920 the combined efforts of the Riley brothers contributed greatly to what was then a fragmented motor industry. Riley was again at the forefront of British car production.

One of my early motoring memories was when I was about eight years old. My parents and I were on holiday in Dorset, staying in a small village near Swanage. Deciding to visit nearby Corfe Castle one day, we set out on what began as a leisurely drive in that direction. The car in question was the new Riley Sports four seater. I remember it as an open car and 'terrifically fast', possibly 65 mph top speed!

'Daddy,' I shouted, *'there's a Standard going to overtake us!'*

The Standard, also made in Coventry, was in my view one of our arch rivals and could not be allowed to steal a march on us in any way. My father must have thought the same for he responded magnificently. Crouching low over the wheel he almost pushed the accelerator through the floor. By this time we were neck and neck, or should it be bonnet and bonnet? Both drivers were obviously getting the last ounce out of their engines. Gradually we started to pull away, but by that time the end of the 'race track' was in sight in the form of a sharp bend. In the back of the other car there was a boy of about my own age. During this marathon we were shaking our fists at one another and mouthing insults (well I know I was). Someone, of course, had to eventually give way before reaching the corner. As we inched forward the driver of the Standard decided to pull back and not before time. As we entered the bend a car emerged from the opposite direction, there were not many inches to spare between us. My mother's comments later that day were;

'Four little boys having a thrilling time and living through it.'

Incidentally, both my mother and father told me off for pulling faces and shaking my fist at the other kid, but I thought it was worth it! At the time, as far as I was concerned, another arch rival was Alvis (another Coventry marque).

'They are very good cars' said my father. *'Impossible'* I thought!

Allan Riley and family members on a Sunday run out with a picnic.

Unfortunately, I do not have many first-hand memories of my grandfather, William Riley, the founder of the Riley Company, but I do remember him as a dynamic, fast talking, fast acting character. At eighty-six years of age he was still in his office every working day as a very active member of the Board, although his eldest son Victor was appointed Managing Director of Riley (Coventry) Limited in 1923. William had unqualified support from his five sons and exerted great influence throughout the many years he was on the Board. They always referred to him as 'The Guv'nor' and were also somewhat in awe of him! With five sons and no daughters he could not afford to be too lenient. He used to call his five sons 'my boys.'

'I'm proud of my boys' he once told me.

He also told my father,

' *You're a lucky man, Allan. Nellie* (my mother) *is a damn fine woman, a lovely woman!'*

In spite of a life devoted to hard work, and also of the fact that he was a heavy smoker, he lived to the ripe old age of ninety-three. My last memory of him was when he was over ninety sitting in an arm chair talking nineteen to the dozen, and surrounded by clouds of cigar smoke. He died in 1944.

With regard to his hard work, enterprise and achievement, his five sons followed in his footsteps very successfully. Sadly, his wife predecesed him by thirty-five years. She died in May, 1909 at the age of fifty-five. My father was then thirty-one. Her death was a terrible blow to the family. She had been revered by her husband and five sons. Through the years she had been a tower of strength, always giving encouragement and sound advice on their many problems. Undoubtedly, along with my grandfather, she was initially responsible for much of the Rileys' success. Hers had been a life of sacrifice. My grandmother had died five years before I was born.

In 1924 my father arrived home one evening looking very happy. We asked him if he had won something on the horses? He gave an emphatic 'No'. (I don't believe he ever placed a bet in his life!). The reason was that the news had just come through that the eleven Riley cars entered in the latest London to Edinburgh run had all arrived without incident, and had all received gold medals awards. No mean achievement in those days!

The activity and character of the five Riley brothers can be best described as follows.

Victor Riley

Chairman and Managing Director of Riley (Coventry) Limited. At the helm of the Riley organisation. Victor was what we called a 'go-getter', he was a brilliant organiser and socialite. Throughout the years, he piloted the Riley companies through some difficult and complex situations with success, and arranged many social and motor sports events on a regular basis. Knowing the right people was a major part of the operation.

Allan Riley

Allan was Managing Director of Midland Motor Bodies Limited, and in some ways, quite different in character from his brother Victor. He was somewhat self-effacing, very astute particularly in financial matters, but shunned the limelight. He worked behind the scenes very effectively and owned many patents in the realm of coach building etc.

Percy Riley

Percy was Managing Director of the Riley Engine Company and originator of Riley engines, including the famous 9hp Riley 'Nine'. Percy was the 'Boffin' of the Riley brothers, and one of the most brilliant motor engineers of his day. He was quietly spoken and also, like my father, shunned publicity.

Stanley Riley

Stanley was a brilliant designer, and was responsible for the body design of most Riley models including the Falcon, and in particular, the streamlined Kestrel. Beside his important position in the Riley organisation, he had two other 'passions'. One was flying, he was a skilled pilot. The other was radio in the early days. He worked hard but he enjoyed the social life as well.

Cecil Riley

Cecil was youngest of the five brothers, and he was universally known as 'Tet'. He worked in various capacities for the company. In his early years he made a name for himself in competition and trials driving. He was a flamboyant, devil-may-care character and joined the army (and later the Royal Flying Corps) in the first World War serving with distinction. After the war he returned to Riley and worked for the Riley Engine Company as a draughtsman and then took the post of Sales Manager for Riley (Coventry) Limited in the early twenties. Towards the end of 1922 Victor Riley, as head of the company, decided to send him to West Africa to assess conditions overseas. What had previously been favourable markets for British cars had suffered a set back, allowing American manufacturers a more or less free market during World War I.
He took a Gold Coast Government job and had many opportunities to observe present trends in American imports. He returned to England in 1926 with information calculated to help the company regain lost ground in Africa. His first job in Coventry was to conduct exhaustive tests on the new Riley '9' prior to its production. Later he was appointed Overseas Sales Manager for

the company. Incidentally, the new '9' became the most popular Riley export to West Africa and other parts of the world. When he set sail for West Africa to take up the Government post, I was about nine years of age at the time, but I remember hearing snatches of conversation in the family about a famous high spirited party at the Adelphi Hotel in Liverpool on the eve of his departure for the Gold Coast. My father thought the celebration went a bit too far, but then he was not an enthusiastic party goer!

The strength and success of the Riley organisation can be attributed to the fact that each of the five brothers used his individual and varied skills with one objective in mind...the success of the Riley car. In other words they were a united family aiming for one target. With one exception they were the only family owned motor company in the country. The brothers seldom used their first names amongst themselves, but were known as AR, (Allan Riley) VR, PR, SR and CR. They were known thus by many people outside the family as well.

Midland Motor Bodies Co. timber store in 1931.

In the earlier years, the Riley Motor Manufacturing Company had been formed with my father as Managing Director. In 1919 the name was changed to Midland Motor Bodies Limited, still under the direction of Allan Riley. It was eventually absorbed as the body division into Riley (Coventry) Limited in 1931. The Riley '9' MkI was built jointly by the Midland Motor Body Company and the Riley Engine Company which was set up by Percy Riley. They were in adjoining premises in Widdrington Road and Aldbourne Road, Coventry. The Riley '9' MkII was built by the Riley Engine Company and Riley (Coventry) Limited.

Although the Riley brothers were, of course, primarily concerned with the design and manufacture of their cars, some in particular were active in other ways. On the publicity/ social side, Victor founded (in 1925) what was to become the world's largest one-car club, The Riley Motor Club and was responsible for 'Concours d'Elégance' in various well known venues, Gleneagles (Perthshire), Eastbourne and Bournemouth. In addition to the Riley Motor Club registered in London, there are Riley Clubs in Scotland, Australia, New Zealand, Ireland, Holland, Sweden, Switzerland and the USA, and all are still flourishing. Victor Riley's son, Victor Riley Jnr., is President of the Riley Register, a club founded in 1954 to foster unthusiasm for pre-Nuffield Rileys.

The Riley stand at the annual London Motor Show was improving year by year. As already mentioned Victor Riley, with brothers Allan and Stanley, were successful in the early days as competition drivers for Riley Tri-cars and later, the new cars. Allan and Percy, however, were mainly devoted to design and production. My father particularly in his younger days, had success in endurance rallies and hill climbs. He was also the family photographer, and took numerous pictures of events in which Riley cars took part, particularly in the years up to World War I competitions with Tri-cars and cars. Later on, Cecil Riley, the youngest of the five brothers had followed suit in competitions himself.

Some of the most important Riley patents were concerned with significant improvements to the internal combustion engine. Percy Riley's patents included; completely new valve mechanisms (mechanically operated inlet valves (1903)); the first continuous mesh gearbox; the 'Silent Third' gearbox.

In the early twenties, the word 'Rileyability' was coined by the company in an advertisement for the side-valve car which was approaching the peak of it's success. It certainly described the qualities the Riley brothers expected from the commencement of their business. In 1925 the famous Riley 'Diamond' trade mark, which had been used since 1920, was introduced with the slogan '**AS OLD AS THE INDUSTRY, AS MODERN AS THE HOUR**'. This was used until the name was acquired by Lord Nuffield in 1938.

In spite of the intensive high pressure activities of the brothers in the manufacture of motor cars there were occasional forays into other realms. Around 1925 Stanley Riley suddenly got bitten by the 'Wireless' bug. I was eleven years old then and became tremendously excited by his lurid description of 'Cats whiskers', crystals, one valve receivers etc.

One warm summer evening in late August he came over from Coventry to our house in the country to install the 'Wireless'. I had been allowed to stay up late to witness all this. Operations started as it was getting dark by the digging of a hole about two foot square by three foot deep in a flower bed in front of the house in what was previously a well ordered and colourful floral display. But then progress marches on! It was explained that to be able to receive any signal at all it was vital to install a good 'earth' to say nothing of a good aerial sited as high as possible.

The day before my father had persuaded our faithful gardener to climb an eighty-five foot Wellingtonia tree to fix the aerial, a hundred foot long wire. The 'first class earth' consisted of a large copper sheet with dozens of small holes punched by hammer and nail. Several cans of water were then poured on it, and the soil, plus remnants of flowers, shovelled back. Uncle Stanley had already mentioned the fact that a good earth should be kept moist for as long as possible, which later prompted my mother to suggest that any male visitor if they felt the need, should go outside and 'water the earth'. Of course, I was duly shocked!

Whilst all this was going on the night sky was illuminated by quite an impressive display of summer lightning. In view of the large copper sheet being handled my mother was rather concerned about the possibility of our house being struck! Unfortunately, by the time the work was completed it was too late to pick up any signal from Daventry 5XX. This was about fifteen miles away and the only station we could receive. Nevertheless, everyone celebrated with drinks all round, but all I was allowed was a lemonade.

We realised the celebration might be somewhat premature as there was no guarantee we would be able to tune into anything. I was too excited to sleep much that night. Just before 10.30am the following morning, everyone gathered round the 'Crystal Set'. Uncle Stanley, who had stayed the night, donned the headphones and started gently scratching the 'Crystal' with the 'Cats Whiskers'. My father looked at me and grinned. Suddenly Stanley shouted.

'Whoops, I've got it! I've got it! Just listen to this!'

There was a mad scramble for the headphones. I got there first. Suddenly I heard a faint voice, then the unmistakable strains of the 'Skaters Waltz'. I thought the whole thing was wonderful and handed the headphones to my mother.

'I can't hear anything,' she said.

There wasn't anything! So Uncle Stanley recommended the crystal scratching and eventually, amongst atmospherics, we heard the 'Daventry Quartet' stepping up the tempo with 'Lonesome and Sorry'. So much for our first radio. Somewhat later when some of the magic had worn off, my mother remarked,

'There's an awful lot of rubbish on this wireless contraption.'

Later on when, when radio became somewhat more complex, she remarked,

'I've never seen so many damn wires in my life. And they call it wireless'

The other radio landmark was when I built my first short wave set and received my first station from across the 'pond' from Schanectady, New York. Again, a string quartet, this time playing 'A Garden In The Rain', my father was most impressed. Also it was one of his favourite tunes.

Still bitten by the radio bug I made a list of the 147 radio stations I had logged over the space of a few days. The Daily Mail at the time was asking children to write in with a list of radio stations they had logged. My mother decided the list should be sent to the Mail. She wrote this out herself, deciding that my childish scrawl was not exactly suitable. A few days later, we were amazed to see a banner headline on an inside page of the paper,

'BOY'S 147 STATIONS'

My nearest rival was a girl of fourteen who had logged just twelve! Of my effort, my father said,

'Quite remarkable.'

I also recall the time I made up a 'two-valve' radio set for an elderly lady which I was proudly explaining how to operate,

'This is the knob for adjusting the volume,' I said.

She was delighted.

'Wonderful. Thank you dear.'

She replied, and continued,

'Where's the thing to make it go fast or slow?'

For a while my father's nickname for me was 'Marconi'. My parents had a great love of music. My father's one regret was that he had no time to study music seriously. He was a self-taught pianist of above average ability. Occasionally he played late into the night. From the age of seven I used to love listening until I fell asleep. After some pleading, my bedroom door was left open. My parents realised it was an effective lullaby! As far as my father was concerned, I am sure this was a therapeutic way to diminish the effects of workday stress.

The same could be said of another of his activities. Very often on a summer evening he could be seen moving in measured, slow steps, rolling what was a considerable expanse of lawn. Whilst on the subject of the garden we were quite self-sufficient in some aspects of food production, including the possession of an extensive kitchen garden and a considerable number of chickens, which brings me to the subject of a screaming pandemonium one Sunday afternoon. I looked out of my window, and there was my father taking huge, rapid strides, covering the ground in record time in the direction of the uproar. It turned out to be a cock fight! My mother remarked later that she'd never seen him move so fast. In fact, his nickname for sometime hence was 'Speedy!'

Quite often, when he returned home in the evening he showed the signs of what had obviously been a hectic day. One of his favourite expressions was,

'Oh, I do feel slack.'

When I first heard this, I was convulsed with giggles. He looked rather hurt.

'What are you laughing at?'

'Nothing', I said.

He looked sternly at me.

'And what do you look like when you're laughing at something?'

Normally, my father did not discuss his business worries at home. He did not like to talk 'shop' unless there was a strong reason. On a particular Sunday morning, there appeared to have been a strong reason. At breakfast he was telling my mother about a business colleague who apparently, had attempted some sharp practice. She had replied with,

'Well, some of it may be your own fault. You may be a good
business man, but you're too trusting at times.'

As the conversation continued animatedly he helped himself to another coffee and a spoonful of sugar. He stirred it thoroughly, put the cup to his lips, and swallowed a copious amount of coffee. Instantaneously, there was a splutter and a yell. He had put his spoon in the mustard pot! It took some time to live that one down.

For a while Victor Riley, then unmarried, stayed with us at the 'Moor House' making the daily six mile trip into Coventry at record speed. There were no limits in those days. We informed him with some amusement tinged with annoyance, that he was the perfect alarm clock sounding off rather too early for my liking! Every morning, Monday to Saturday, at precisely seven o'clock, we heard rapid footsteps towards the bathroom with subsequent slamming of the door and loud sound of ablutions, gargling etc. Equally loud sound of descent to the breakfast room. Fifteen minutes later, sound of front door slamming, then sound of starter roar of engine and exhaust, then he was away at breakneck speed.

On one particular morning just along the lane from the house, he rounded a sharp bend and was confronted by a gang of roadmen and a steam roller taking up most of the road. He pointed the car between the steam roller and the grassy bank thinking he could make it, then realised he couldn't. It was too late to stop. He crashed through the gap slicing off all four wings which were left lying in the road. 'Mudguards' in those days, which tended to stick out from the body somewhat! He had no intention of stopping, he would have been late at the office, so he left four bemused roadmen staring after the car. Later that morning a driver from the works was sent out to pick up the debris.

Another amusing story concerning Victor was the time he was staying with Percy and Norah Riley. Early one morning, even earlier than usual, they heard frenzied footsteps making for the front door. Norah saw him about to open the door, his shirt tails flapping, no tie and hair unruly. He was always known for his immaculate business attire. She called out,

'Victor, you're not dressed properly and you haven't had your breakfast.'

'Sorry, can't help that,' he shouted back.

*'I've just thought of something. Got to get to the office. **FAST!**'*

What the dire emergency was, I never found out.

The only day in the week I looked forward to with mixed feelings was Sunday. We were all happy to have my father at home on that day, but the trouble was he loved walking in the countryside and I did not! I tried to make every excuse to avoid this and in desperation, resorted to hiding in cupboards, the cellar, anywhere, but he always found me, so I resigned myself to making the best of it.

During these walks, he often regaled me with stories of his younger days, and in time, I began to actually enjoy the walks.

One of his more amusing stories was when he was in London to attend a business conference. He was not used to London traffic and it was a boiling hot day in July. He was driving through Piccadilly Circus, wearing a large, floppy Panama hat. Suddenly, he almost collided with a taxicab. There was a screech of brakes as the cabby yelled out,

'Cor blimey, Guv, you're not in the middle of the bleedin' Sahara Desert!'

In 1925 the new Riley '9' was completed. After exhaustive road and endurance tests all over the UK and also in the Alps, it was launched in 1926, in time for that year's motor show. The engine featured Percy Riley's new 'PR' cylinder head, with overhead valve mechanism.

The demise of the side valve was now in sight. The gearbox had a 'silent 3rd' which was a considerable improvement on previous units. Easier gear change was also a feature of the new gearbox. In this range was included the first fabric bodied model, the 'Monaco', which became very popular.

1934 Riley 9hp Monaco.
(Publicity Photo)

Later there was also the Riley '9' 'Biarritz', and a six cylinder saloon, the 'Edinburgh', named after the successful London to Edinburgh runs.

1927 Riley 11.9hp Chatsworth Saloon.

At the 1927 Motor Show, amongst an impressive display of Riley cars, were the 9hp 'San Remo' and 'Monaco' saloons originating from my father's coach building company. He was justly proud of those cars. Two highlights in my father's year were the London and Paris motor shows. As far as I remember he was accompanied either by brother Victor or Stanley. Obviously great benefit was derived from exhibiting their cars at Olympia. The Paris show was viewed as a combined business activity to assess the European market and also savour the lighter side of life, particularly the food! On one particular occasion my father was very impressed by a famous Russian restaurant on the Champs Elysées. The waiters attired in Georgian army uniform, served enormous steaks on the end of a highly ornate sword. He assured me he was perfectly sober at the time!

Towards the end of the twenties with engines becoming ever more efficient and faster, particular attention was given to the car's braking system. It was at that time that four wheel brakes were introduced. However, some drivers were unprepared for a car's increased stopping power by adding a braking system to the front wheels, so a timely warning was given to the driver behind in the form of a red triangle fixed on the rear of the car with the legend *'FOUR WHEEL BRAKES'* inscribed on the three sides.

1931 Motor Show showing the 1932 models.

1929 and 1930 were very successful years for Riley. Apart from winning many motor sport trophies, there was great success on the financial side. In 1930 there was a grand celebration at a distributors' luncheon at the Savoy Hotel in London on the 'Historic occasion of the season's sales of the company passing the £1,000,000 mark'. A vast amount in those days. Among the many distinguished guests were Captain Malcolm Campbell, the Rt. Hon. the Earl of March and Sir Edward Manville JP. The five Riley brothers were there, and it must have been a very proud moment. My father didn't say much about it, but my mother and I could tell from the warmth in his voice that it was something he would never forget. He had every reason to be proud of his contribution to the success of Riley cars, but he was content to contribute and remain quietly in the background.

In the late twenties and early thirties, I took a great interest in endurance trials and hill climbs in which Riley excelled. They had great successes at the Shelsley Walsh hill climb in Worcestershire. The steepest gradient on the course was one in three, upon which many of the contestants became unstuck. In the summer of 1926 the new Riley 'Monaco' designed by Stanley Riley made its first appearance at the venue and attracted much attention.

Riley Motor Club North East Centre Rally.
Mr S.H.Roe on Park Rash in his Riley 9hp Gamecock in the mid thirties.

As far back as 1909 Victor Riley won the Members' Event at Shelsley and the Club Cup at the Aston Clinton Hill Climb. Riley were also second in both events. My father also scored successes at Shelsley Walsh in 1909. In 1929, Riley 9's won all seven categories, and also took the President's Cup. Unfortunately, owing to my ill health, it was not normally possible for me to take an active part in what were such exciting years for the Riley family between 1925 and 1935.

Over the years, many people have asked me what the Riley brothers and their families were really like when they were at home, away from the activity and pressures of their daily work. I think the answer should be,

'Like most other families.'

A mixture of imponderables. When I was young, one of my father's catch phrases on leaving for the office in Coventry was,

'Well, I'm off now to the city of laughter and tears.'

Surely a good description of family life? Appertaining to 'Family', the five Riley brothers were, in order of seniority,

Victor Riley

Victor was the socialite of the five brothers. He was largely responsible for organising numerous events and competitions such as trials, rallies, road and track racing, 'Concours d'Elégance' and was president of the Riley Motor Club, for many years the world's largest one car club. The Riley Record, the club's bimonthly magazine, was first published in 1927. His wife Dorothy née Champney was a well known rally and racing driver who, in 1934, clocked up the then fastest time ever achieved by any woman driver at Le Mans. Victor and Dorothy led an active home life along with their two children Victor and Victoria. In later years, they lived in a luxuriously appointed house in the Cotswolds, entertaining lavishly.

Allan Riley

Allan was mainly concerned with the coach building side of the business, and apart from his numerous early successes as a competition and trials driver, was also responsible for no less than 37 patents mainly concerned with body and chassis design.

In 1934, six Riley cars were entered for the famous Le Mans 24 Hour race, and all six finished. They won the 1100cc and 1500cc classes team prize. And the Riley '9' 'Brooklands' won the Rudge Whitworth cup. I remember a celebration at the Moor House as a result. Victor Riley was there, and I think, Stanley as well. My father allowed me a small sip of his Guinness, his favourite tipple at the time. My mother looked slightly concerned, but there was no need to worry because I thought it tasted horrible!

1934 was the year that Riley fitted the ENV pre-selector gearbox, the gear selector lever being fixed to the steering column. This, of course, was a complete departure from the normal gate change. Gone were the days of double de-clutching and gear crashing! Of the Riley brothers, my father and Percy Riley topped the patents list, around 37 each. In Percy's case, most were, of course, concerning engine and gearbox design. My mother enjoyed acting as hostess for various family and business functions, and coped very successfully. She did not drive, and as she remarked, preferred to leave that sort of thing to the Riley men. One of her quips was,

> *'Outside every pub there was almost bound to be a Riley car. If there wasn't,*
> *there must be something wrong either with the pub, or the beer!'*

She was an outgoing person in contrast to my father's quiet and somewhat serious disposition. Different in temperament, yes, but happily married! She was born in India, her father was a Captain in the British Army. On his retirement, he and his wife went to live in Lausanne, Switzerland, and ended their days there. Obviously, my mother loved the social life, and at times, found the Moor House somewhat lonely, with my father being so busily occupied with the Riley organisation.

Percy Riley

Percy was married to Norah and their three daughters, Patricia, Gillian and Rosalind, took an active interest in the family business as they grew up. Gillian, joined the motor sport fraternity.

With his amazing output of invention and design in engineering, Percy Riley influenced and enriched not only the future of the British Motor Industry, but also that of foreign companies. In spite of such an active life, he managed to find time for some social activity. Every Christmas Day, he and Norah organised the family reunion with normal attendance at twenty or more! Invariably, my father was expected to play the piano. Needless to say, he needed no encouragement!

As a wedding present for his wife, Percy designed and built their house in the country near Warwick. He lived there for the rest of his life. He died in 1941 at the age of fifty-eight. A genius, responsible for the design of many Riley engines and gearboxes, from the first car in 1898.

Stanley Riley

Stanley was married with one son, Ivan. In World War II, Ivan joined the Fleet Air Arm, and had the perilous job of ferrying planes from Canada to the war zone in France. Along with my father, Stanley was responsible for the design of famous Riley models such as the 'Kestrel', 'Monaco' and 'Falcon'.

1935 Riley 1½ litre Kestrel. Two young ladies finding another use for the car.

As early as 1906 to 1909, he was very successful in winning competitions at the wheel of cars of his own design.

Cecil ('Tet') Riley

As already mentioned, Cecil Riley was very active and successful in various company activities. His wife Billie, was well known as a competition driver of Riley cars.

'Tet' Riley (Riley Imp) with the Mayor of Aberystwyth on Lead Mines Hill during preliminary investigations of the 1935 Riley '24 Hour' Trial.

I remember my father being involved in what might have been a fatal accident. He was test driving the new 1928 Chatsworth saloon, (nicknamed 'The Greenhouse', owing to the large expanse of window glass) on the busy Coventry to Birmingham road, and was just overtaking a lorry and trailer, when the outfit jack-knifed. The end of the trailer came into violent contact with the offside of his car, shattering the three windows. The interior of the car was covered in glass fragments. Mercifully, he was only slightly injured, although badly shaken. There was no safety glass in those days. In 1934 Triplex safety glass was fitted as standard on all Riley cars, years before most other manufacturers followed suit.

Around 1931 there was great excitement at home. We had purchased a model of the first television set manufactured for the home market. This was the John Logie Baird receiver, consisting of a large revolving disc suitably masked apart from a small vertical 'window' about the size of half a postcard, which displayed a faint, flickering image in two shades of orange. The announcer cried excitedly,

'And now, see and hear the one act play by Luigi Pirandello,'

'The Flowers Are Not For You To Pick'

The 'image' consisted of a vague figure flitting about, and someone waving an unrecognisable flower in front of the camera. The tinny dialogue did not help matters and also the strain appeared to be too much for the equipment, which started overheating producing a smell of smouldering rubber. Although my father was suitably impressed by another marvel of modern technology, his sense of humour eventually took over. He christened the thing 'smellyvision'.

In 1932 a certain Freddie Dixon decided to try his hand at car racing. He was already well known in the 1920's for achieving considerable success in motor cycle racing. He then joined the Riley Team, and later became a Riley legend with outstanding successes at Brooklands, Le Mans, Montlhery, the Ulster TT and other important venues. My father knew him as a 'wild man', a terrific character, but above all, a great racing driver.

As an antidote for speed, in March 1934 the 30 mph speed limit was introduced in towns and built-up areas in the UK.

Freddy Dixon pictured at the British Empire Trophy in 1935 at Brooklands.

There was uproar for a time, but before long most people realized that in view of the ever increasing volume of traffic on the roads, this new law was a necessity. Going back to the very early years of motoring, (around 1896) no motorised vehicle was allowed on the highways unless preceded by a man ponderously walking along the road waving a red flag! However, this absurd law did not last long, but was succeeded by the imposition of a 12mph speed limit. Almost as frustrating.

In 1935 which was a busy and very successful year for Riley cars, my father was medically advised to take a break, having endured months of stressful work. What better place than South Africa to test out the new 'Falcon' and make acquaintance with the growing number of Riley owners and enthusiasts over there? (The same thing was happening in Australia). He decided that this trip must be a family affair, so my mother and I accompanied him. Who were we to argue?

We sailed from Tilbury Docks in the 10,000 ton SS 'City of Paris'. Our car was duly hoisted on board by crane from the dockside. None of your easy 'drive on, drive off' facilities. I had just been issued with an International Driving Licence, so was raring to go! The comparatively small boat did not stand us in good stead for crossing the Bay of Biscay which is rough at the best of times, but when there is a violent storm which there was, forget it! My father however, was never affected by the roughest seas.

The morning after the storm he calmly sauntered along to the dining room for breakfast. There were only two other people there. The total should have been around fifty. My mother and I had just about recovered when we docked in Cape Town.

However one incident did cheer us up during the latter part of the voyage. A certain passenger who had dabbled in amateur dramatics, rounded up a number of people he thought would be suitable to act in a play he had recently written. He chose my father to be one of the leading characters although he had never acted in his life, not even in the school play. He was to take the part of a character who found himself in the dock accused of being drunk and disorderly, and was in fact, still under the influence! Rehearsals got under way, and in a few days, the 'play' had it's premier in what was grandly called the 'Ship's Theatre'. He was the hit of the evening, giving a masterful performance. My mother agreed that whilst he was good, it was not really *him*. I asked her to explain. She said,

"Drunk, maybe. Disorderly, never!"

The holiday as I saw it, was an experience indeed. In those days, outside the towns good roads were almost non existent. In some areas due to alternate blistering heat and heavy rainfall, the corrugated surface of the road was extremely punishing to tyres and suspension, but the car stood up manfully.

We covered a considerable amount of terrain during our South African trip from our base in Cape Town. Places such as East London, Port Elizabeth, Pietermaritzburg, Durban and Mossel Bay in Cape Province.

My father visited Johannesburg and the Riley agent there, who reported record sales for that year. I decided to make full use of my International Driving Licence and did a lot of the driving, encouraged by my father. One incident however, was too much. A small road in the wilds of Natal crossed a partially dried-up river bed which we were in the process of negotiating. Unfortunately an invisible submerged rock made short work of the sump. There we were in mid stream with no oil left in the engine! The outcome was an eventual tow in to Durban twenty-five miles distant and ten days wait for a new sump. We recounted all this to Stanley Riley when we returned home, but his reply was,

> *'If you'd been there when I was, you'd have hardly found anything you would call roads, even in the towns.'*

Stanley had been to South Africa on a sales promotion and test drive many years before. Both my parents and I were gratified by the interest shown in this new Riley model (Falcon).

Riley cars had already achieved fame over the years with a 1932 9hp model setting the 'Durban to Johannesburg' record. In 1933, a Riley Six set the Johannesburg/Durban/Durban/Johannesburg record time of 18 hours, 12 minutes. In 1937, a year after our visit, Rileys were 2nd and 3rd in the South African Grand Prix, and a year later came in 1st and 3rd.

In spite of the great success and consolidation of the Riley companies over the preceding twenty five years or so, by the end of November 1937, due to various circumstances some unavoidable, trading conditions suddenly worsened. However' one factor which was responsible for considerable additional expenditure was the ambitious launch in 1937 of Autovia Cars Limited as part of the Riley group. The engine was a V8. This was the largest car Riley had produced, and was in the luxury limousine class. Unfortunately, early sales did not come up to expectations, and this proved the final straw. The Directors had to announce a trading loss, but it was hoped that profits placed in reserve in previous years would cover this. Unfortunately, conditions became even more difficult, and in February 1938, a receiver and manager was appointed to run the affairs of the company until its sale to Lord Nuffield in September. The events of that year had a profound effect on my father. Here was what had been a thriving family car business achieving success in quality, reliability, performance and comfort with equal success in motor sports. Some of the better known Riley competition successes from 1900 to 1938, when the company was owned entirely by the Riley family, totalled around 443.

The 1938 Autovia.

In East Africa in 1926 a Riley '12' Tourer made the first car journey from Nairobi to Mombassa. Other rivals attempted the same thing, but failed to complete the course. In 1927 in the Australian 700 Mile Alpine Tour, two Riley 9's were joint first. In 1929 in the AustralianTrans Continental run, (Fremantle to Sydney) a Riley '9' covered the 2850 miles in five days, eight hours, a record. In 1930, another Riley '9' established another record, covering the ground from New York to Los Angeles, a distance of 4250 miles averaging 41 mph. In 1931 in the German 10,000km Trial, two Riley 9's won first class awards.In the Australian 200 mile Grand Prix, a Riley '9' was overall first, also creating a lap record.

Now this company was going out of the hands of a family who had worked so hard for the good name of their product and that of the motor industry for the last forty years. In the forty years to 1938, the Riley family company sold 60,200 cars. The 9hp Riley 'Nine' was the most popular model with sales in excess of 28,000. In the early years between 1904 and 1907, Riley 9hp engines were supplied for the South African and Tasmanian governments to power rail cars on the national railway systems. In the early thirties the company produced a series of very successful marine engines. 1935 saw the Riley '9' fitted with the new Armstrong Siddeley pre-selector gearbox. Also in that year, a new four cylinder 1½ litre engine was introduced.

This powered an advanced style streamlined saloon, and was the forerunner of what became the famous Riley 1½ litre saloon. The three years, from 1935 to 1938 had resulted in the company producing a wide range of new models, which imposed an increased financial burden on the organisation, but without the debacle of the Autovia 'adventure', things might have been very different. I knew my father had been truly worried for months, but being the sort of man he was, he kept most of this to himself. The signs were there, lack of sleep, restlessness, the disappointments, the stress of trying to be optimistic. I know his brothers felt the same, but my worry of course, was mainly for my father. I shall always remember his words after the company was dissolved.

'The Riley cars were made to last...and so will the name Riley.'

Another great sadness in our lives had been the death of my mother in 1936, from which my father was just beginning to recover. She had recently returned from our holiday in South Africa, and was visiting her parents in Switzerland, when she contracted double pneumonia.

In early 1939 to gain engineering experience, I took a job with the Bristol Aeroplane Company in the Inspection Department (Standards Room). Later that year, when war clouds appeared to be gathering, I told my father that I was volunteering for the Navy, but he said that I would not be released from Bristol. He was right, so, like my father in the First World War I was in a reserved occupation for the duration of hostilities. We certainly experienced some hectic moments like most other people in Britain, but our plight was not to be compared to those heroes in the battle zones.

In August 1940, the Luftwaffe pin-pointed the two BAC factories in Bristol in a massive air raid with unfortunately, heavy loss of life. A bomb fell about five yards from the 'mushroom' shelter I was in, but thankfully no one in our shelter was even injured, although naturally very shaken. I had a Riley 12/4 Kestrel at the time, which did not escape the bombs. A few minutes after the 'all clear' sounded, those of us with cars, which were in the majority, rushed out to the adjoining car park to see what was left of them. One or two were complete wrecks. I was somewhat luckier. The boot and petrol tank on the Kestrel were shattered, and a couple of tyres blown, otherwise, not too bad! Whilst we were all still looking at our individual wreckage, a voice screamed,

'LOOK OUT! GET DOWN!'

The next second two planes zoomed at terrific speed over our heads at what appeared to be a few hundred feet from the ground. Convinced it was curtains for us, we threw ourselves on to the tarmac. We later learned the planes were a couple of Hurricane patrol fighters from the nearby BAC airfield. With the help of some fellow workers, I managed to make my Riley more or less roadworthy, minus the petrol tank.

We overcame the problem by rigging up a five gallon drum on the passenger seat with a gravity feed via a small rubber tube to the carburettor! In that way, I limped up to the Riley (Nuffield) factory in Coventry for the necessary repairs, accompanied by an all pervading smell of petrol fumes. I was longing for a cigarette, correction, cigarettes, but decided I'd had enough near misses already without setting in motion what would surely be the final curtain!

A Riley 12/4 Kestrel during the bombing of Coventry outside Boots the Chemist in November 1940.

When I arrived back at the factory, I did create some interest. A Riley car back from the UK front line! Coventry had yet to experience the awful devastation which occurred later. When my father saw me and the car with the 'live' petrol drum on the passenger seat next to mine, he was quite overcome.

'Are you sure you're alright?'

'Never fitter!', I replied, grinning.

But I still got a reprimand.

'That was a damned silly thing to do. You could have blown yourself sky high.'

But of course, I would have the last word.

'I don't think it was', I said, *'And to prove it, I'm here.'*

He gave up! I'm sure he said to himself,

'I wouldn't have been such a bloody fool when I was his age!'

In some ways, I suppose it could have been good publicity for the car! A picture of it appeared in the local paper.

The next afternoon I was on the train bound for Bristol. When we got to Mangotsfield Junction, about 10 miles from Bristol, an announcement was made to the effect that owing to a heavy air raid on the town, the train would proceed no further. In fact, we could see almost continuous flashes in the night sky and the red glow of what must have been massive fires. We could also hear the rumble of exploding bombs and anti-aircraft fire. We eventually arrived at Temple Meads Station in Bristol at 4.30 am. On my walk from the station and along Park Street, the main thoroughfare, there were scenes of desolation, shattered and burning buildings. I could hear occasional explosions around the city, presumably time bombs detonating.

As I was passing some hoardings in Park Street, there was a massive explosion behind them, and debris crashed against the boards. Fortunately for me, they withstood the shock. I eventually reached the digs in Clifton to find other inmates, including some of my friends, still sheltering in the cellar. When they knew what I'd done, one of them said caustically,

'There's one born every minute!'

Later that morning, an urgent call came through from my father enquiring if I was alright.

'Of course I am.' I replied.

Sadly, three of my friends who worked at the Filton offices half a mile away were killed when their shelter received a direct hit. The fatal casualties were ninety people. Such was the devastation that it was not possible to identify the bodies.

A Scottish colleague of mine in the Bristol Aeroplane Company known to everyone as, 'Mac', who else?, was the proud owner of a Riley '9' Monaco. He called it

'A wonderful wee machine.'

One bitterly cold ice bound night in the winter of 1942, we had just partaken of a few 'jars' of ale in the local, and were on our way back to our wartime digs along a country lane, when we got into a monumental skid. The Riley shot off the road, cut a swathe through a copse of bushes and small trees and ended up with the front end overhanging a deep drop to a large, ice covered pond. We were literally balanced on a knife edge, and sat stock still until we had recovered from the shock. Then Mac said quietly,

'For God's sake, get over to the back seat.'

We made our way as if treading on eggshells. Suddenly the car started rocking alarmingly, but then, mercifully, the front tipped up. We both scrambled out of the offside rear door.

'Bloody hell!!' gasped Mac.

'If she hadn't been so tough, we might have been crushed to death or drowned!'

During the war years 1940/45, Riley Coventry (Successors) Limited, was working full time on the production of war vehicles and munitions. Car production resumed late in 1945 with a new 1½ litre model. This was a sleek lined saloon which became very popular. Incidentally, along with the 'Kestrel', it was my father's favourite car. Riley Coventry (Successors) Limited subsequently became part of the British Motor Corporation, formed in 1953. Victor Riley remained as Managing Director of Riley Coventry Ltd. He died in 1958 at the age of eighty-two after a life of achievement through hard work and brilliant organisation, becoming head of the company in the early twenties. My cousin, Victor William is now President of the Riley Motor Club, (and the Riley Register) and works as his father did, for its continued success. He and his wife Elizabeth, still travel (in 2002) world wide to attend various Riley functions, including the recent celebrations in Australia for the Centenary of the Riley car.

In 1954 the Riley Register Club was formed. The object was to bring together the owners of Riley cars built between 1900 and 1938, when the company was entirely family owned.

In 1961 we mourned the death of Cecil (Tet) Riley. In his sixty-severn years, his zest for life had brought him many successes. His activities in the Riley organisation have already been mentioned, but he also served with distinction in World War I. He joined the army as a despatch rider and later, commissioned in the field, he joined the Royal Flying Corps as an observer, and finally, a pilot.

It is interesting to note that the Riley '9' engine produced by Percy Riley in 1925, which later on earned that model the name 'that wonder car' was still in production thirteen years later. In fact eighteen years after the company had been sold to Lord Nuffield in 1938, Riley stayed in the Nuffield group until Austin/Nuffield merged to form BMC. Tragically today, (2003) around 90% of the UK motor industry is in foreign hands.

During the war years, my father continued to live at the Moor House, in almost solitary existence since the death of his wife, my mother. The house was eventually sold, and he then moved into an apartment in Kenilworth. In spite of the irreplaceable loss of the Riley business, he was fortunate to have connections with two firms, Bradite Limited paint manufacturers in Bethesda, North Wales, of which he became a director and subsequently, Chairman, and Gears (Burbage) Limited near Hinckley. He was a Director of the firm, along with Norah Riley. I subsequently joined the board.

At the end of the war, I left the Bristol Aeroplane Company, and my father 'talked me into' (I offered no opposition!) rejoining the 'family'. I took a sales training course, and was then appointed Bradite sales representative for Lancashire and Cheshire. Later, I was appointed a Director.

I well remember the day about a month after I had started work, that my father came up to Manchester where I had digs, to see me and assess the lay of the land. Neither of us were prolific letter writers so the visits to each other were our way of keeping in touch! As petrol was still in short supply, I suggested that to see the town, there was no better way than to take a bus. He would get a panoramic view of Manchester. He looked rather surprised, and didn't seem too keen to get this view of Manchester, but finally agreed. So we boarded a double-decker.

'Shall we go upstairs?' I asked.

He looked quite apprehensive and replied,

'I'm not going up there!'

But with some gentle persuasion, he agreed. When we reached the top deck, he sat down, then looked out of the window and down at the street, saying with some alarm,

'It's a long way down!'

I assured him it was perfectly safe. Then we set off across Piccadilly, the main square, larger and more imposing than London's Piccadilly Circus. All was well until we zoomed up behind another double-decker bus.

'*LOOK OUT!*', he shouted,

and slammed his foot hard down on an imaginary brake, much to the amusement of other passengers! However, tension was somewhat reduced when at the far end of Piccadilly, he spotted four quite large palm trees set in huge tubs.

'Palm trees in Manchester?' he said. *'I ask you!'*

No doubt someone's idea of brightening up the air of post-war shabbiness. It would have looked more natural in Torquay!

Another amusing incident was the time my father arrived at Bethesda for the Bradite monthly board meeting. It was a bitterly cold winter's day with snow on the ground. George Edwards, the Managing Director, was waiting with Ernest Chidley, his fellow Director, for the arrival of the Chairman. They were gazing out at the snowy scene on the imposing entrance to the office block, when a brand new Riley 1½ litre glided into view.

'Look out!', cried George Edwards, *'Here's the Chairman!'*

My father got out of the car, and sauntered slowly towards the office, in his shirt sleeves.

'What the devil's happened to him?' gasped George, *'He must be off his head!'*

When the man of the moment entered the office, Ernest remarked,

'You must be freezing?'

'Not at all', replied the Chairman. *'I'm as warm as toast. Come and have a look.'*

He took them out to the car and pointed to what looked like a small loudspeaker suspended from the dashboard. It was an early 'Electric' car heater, worked entirely from the battery. Tough on the battery!

Incidentally my father delivered the first post-war Riley car (a 1½ litre) in North Wales to Colonel Whowell in Abersoch. His son Frederick became a director of the company after the retirement of George Edwards.

Another seasonable story concerning my father, happened the same winter at a hotel on Anglesey, where at the time, central heating was not one of the amenities. He normally stayed there when attending board meetings in Bethesda. Frederick Whowell wanted to discuss some company policy before the meeting took place, and gave him an early call at the hotel. He went to his room, and knocked the door.

'Come in,' called a faint voice.

Frederick opened the door, and was met with clouds of steam.

'Pop!', he shouted in alarm. *'Where are you?'*

'Over here,' replied the voice.

Through the steam he saw my father calmly sitting in an armchair, reading the Financial Times.

'What on earth's going on?,' gasped Frederick.

'I'll tell you,' replied Pop. *'This is the only way I can keep warm in this damn place!'*

The steam was coming from the washbasin, which he had filled with near boiling water. With due reverence, he was known by a number of people in Bethesda as 'Pop'.

Frederick also recalled one memorable evening around Christmas time at one of the local pubs, when 'Pop' was as usual, playing the piano. Once he started it was sometimes difficult to get him to stop, especially near closing time! In this particular instance, he was giving a spirited rendering of 'March of the Gladiators'. Such was the enthusiasm of the crowd, that they formed a line and started the Conga, which grew and grew in length, emerging from the front door, snaking round the building, and re-entering through the back door! And this kept happening! He was adept at playing by ear and had a repertoire of popular tunes, also some of his own compositions, one in particular, he called a 'March' which was much in demand. It *was* a good tune!

As he approached his eighty-fourth year, my father's health began to deteriorate, and as a result he decided to give up driving. His life had been devoted to motor cars so this was a very bitter pill to swallow, but I suppose it was a wise decision, although after that he more or less gave up. He died in 1963, at the age of eighty-five. He was responsible for many facets of the company's activities and successes, and was a valued financial advisor. In the realm of coachwork, he was responsible for many patents which helped Riley to keep ahead of their competitors.

The last of the Riley Brothers. As many people said,

'He was a real gentleman.'

A fitting epitaph.

And now that BMW own the Riley name, they have it in their power to launch a quality car on world markets. Hopefully Riley may yet survive. I often think about the contribution made by my grandfather, his five sons and all the people who worked for them. Contributors to the birth of the motor car.

Something to be proud of.

The Early Years (1896-1928)

My Mother and Father at my Christening.

A close up picture of Moor House near Fillongley, Coventry.

Original Trade-Mark
of the Riley Cycle Co

The manufacture of Riley pedal cycles started in 1890 and ceased in 1911. The cycle illustrated here was one of the last to be produced.

'I will ride there and you can ride back!'

(Above) 1905 4.5 hp Riley water-cooled Tri-car.

1905 Riley 6hp De Luxe Tri-car. (Original price was £126.0s)

349

1907 Riley 9hp V-Twin. Original price £168.0s.

1907 Riley 12/8hp V-Twin.

1912 Riley 12/18hp Long Wheel Base with Torpedo body.

1911 Riley 12/18hp.

A test run in 1912 in the Riley 12/18.

1912 Riley 10 hp two seat Torpedo.

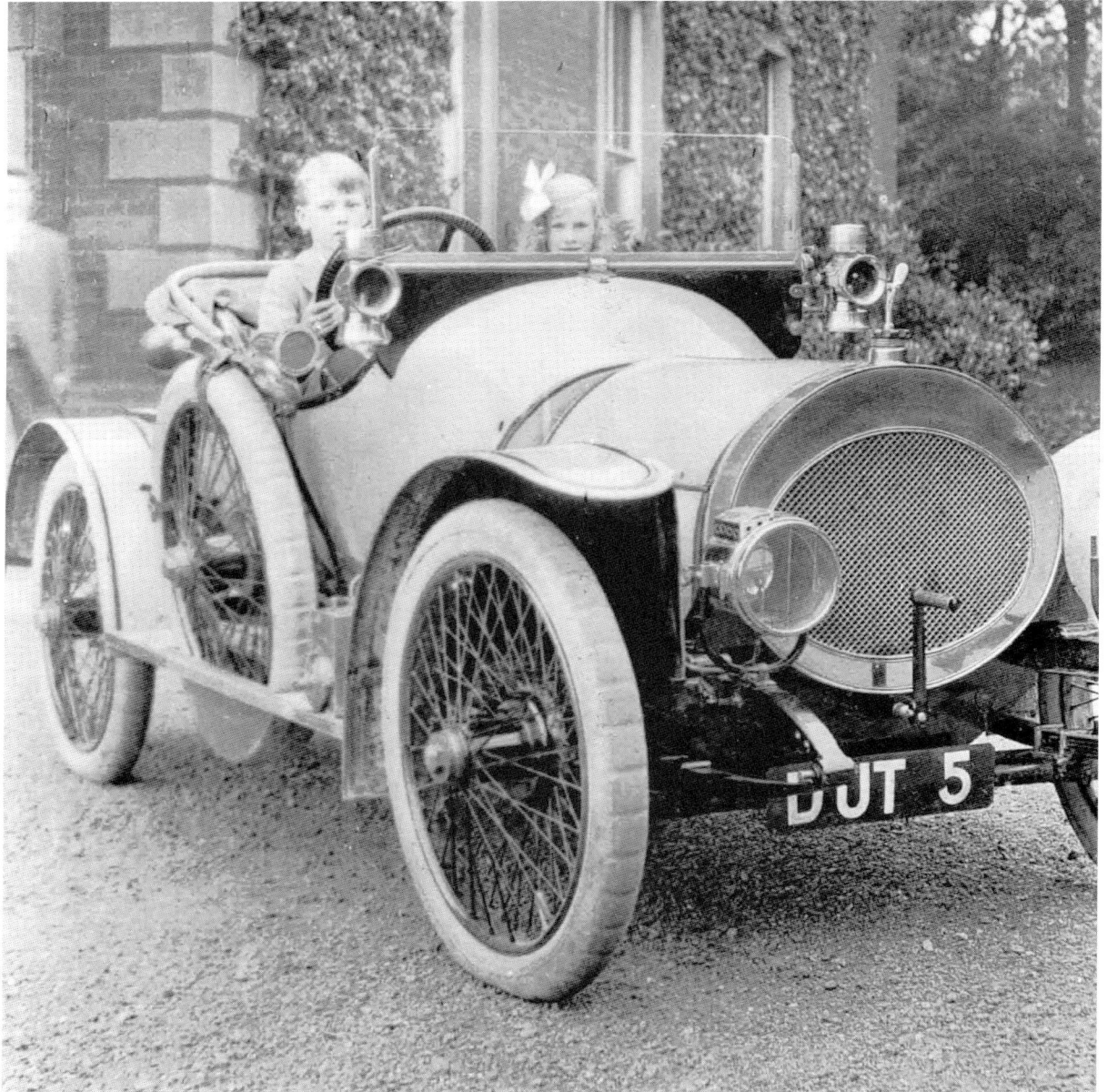

1911 Riley 12/18 Short Wheelbase.
Here I am sitting at the wheel of my dad's test car. I was very excited.

1908 Riley 12/18 two seater.

1909 Riley 10 hp Speed Model.

A 1909 Riley 10hp during manoeuvres used by the Army authorities.
(Seen here driven by Stanley Riley)

1908/09 Riley 10hp 2 seater works car.

'Is there something wrong with your Riley my dear?'

A young lady filling her 1909 Riley 10hp SWB.

1922 Riley (All-Season)
10.8 four seater.

1926 Riley 11/40
four seater.

1922 Riley 11/40 Sports.

1924 Sidevalve Riley
11hp Tourer.

1928 Riley 9hp Fabric Tourer four seater.

'How will I explain this to my husband?'

1924 Riley 10.8 2 seater Redwinger.

*The late Mr Rose from Cheltenham and Jim Robson discussing the prowess
of the Redwinger.*

Richard Riley seen here standing proudly next to a friend's Riley 1½ litre Kestrel.

Complimentary
Lunch
to
Riley (Coventry) Ltd.

Savoy
Hotel
14:1:30

W. Slingsby Esq.

The Organising Committee
of the
London Distributors
of the
RILEY CAR
request the pleasure of your company
at a
COMPLIMENTARY LUNCH
to
RILEY (COVENTRY) LTD.
on the
Historic Occasion of the Season's Sales
of the Company passing the
£1,000,000 mark

Rendez-vous
Savoy Hotel

R.S.V.P

Jan. 14th
12-45 p.m.

Two pictures showing the menu and tickets given to the Distributors. The reason for the lunch was that the Riley Company had passed the £1,000,000 sales mark in one season and had also been in existence for forty years. The event took place at the Savoy Hotel, London in 1930.

*1904 Riley 4.5hp
water cooled Tri-car.*

*1911 Riley 2 seat SWB
12/18hp.*

1934 Riley 14/6 Gamecock.
Alpine Trial Team Car.

1924 Riley 10.8 2 seater Redwinger (Sandracer)

A modified Riley Sprite 1½ litre.

A Riley Ascot 9hp cooling off.

A fine example of a Riley RM 1½ litre.

A Riley RM 2½ litre Drophead Coupé.

A Riley RM 1½ litre very proud of its badges.

A Riley Pathfinder with an unusual number plate.

A nice 1966 Riley 4/72 seen from both the front and rear.

Two splendid examples of the Riley One-Point-Five.

A very fine example of a 1967 Riley Elf Mk III.

This photograph shows the final resting place of a number of the Riley family. The location is the old original main cemetery near the centre of Coventry.

As you can see the Celtic Cross, after being declared dangerous some years ago by Coventry City Council, has been lain on its main base for safety reasons.

Allan Riley was laid to rest in a cemetery on the Radford Road on the Northwest side of the City. The Radford Road would have been the route he would have taken to and from the factory from his home at Moor House near Fillongley.

Competition and Production
(1929-1938)

Riley 11-40hp winner of the 1924 handicap at Brooklands at 81.63 mph.
Driver Victor Gillow.

H.W.Purdy 500 Kilometre and 500 Mile World Record 1928 9hp Riley.

The 1932 Belfast T.T.
The Riley pits including Ian Finwick, 'Tet' Riley and Blackburn.
All very serious.

26th August 1932 TT.
Eyston (16) and Whitcroft (17) seen here at the start of the Ulster Tourist Trophy
at Ards in their Riley '9' Brooklands.

Eyston (16) followed by Whitcroft (17) in 1932 TT.

Gillow (22) follows Eyston (16) again at 1932 TT.
(Whitcroft was to win)

The British Racing Drivers Club 500 mile race at Brooklands on September 24th 1932.

The 1932 British 1,000 mile race at Brooklands.
Miss Joan Richmond at speed during the race in which she won with Mrs Elsie Wisdom.

Ladies checking their own car before the start of the 1932 Monte Carlo Rally.

1933 Riley 6/12 holder of World Record Class F.

1934 Le Mans 24 hour race.

(Riley pits)

1934 June 16th and 17th Le Mans 24 hour race.

1934 F.W.Dixon with his Riley 12/6 at (White House) LeMans.

1934 Riley pits at Le Mans. (Racing MPH)

Dorothy Champney and Kay Petre at the end of the Le Mans 24 hour race in 1934.

Dorothy Champney seen here during the race.

1934 Le Mans.
A racing MPH driven by
Jean Sebilleau and George de la Roche.
2nd Overall, 1st in Class F.

1934 Brooklands 500.
Streamlined Brooklands '6' in sharp duel with an Alfa Romeo and a Bugatti.

A.W.K. Von der Becke.
(Riley Brooklands '9')

T.H.Wisdom.
(Riley Brooklands '9')

The 1935 Monte Carlo Rally.
Car worship. Typical of the crowds which gathered around the competitors in Southern Italy. They all wanted to help.

Sunny Italy? Soon after Rome it became necessary to fit chains in order to get up the main road hills. The two cars in the background did not get beyond this point.

Leaving Italy, the snow gradually thickened. There was worse to come.

1935 Monte Carlo Rally. Heading for Padua we encoutered a very severe blizzard. There were 92 miles to be covered in conditions like this. Fourteen cars failed to get through at all and others struggled through, hours late. At this point they were forced to lower the hood and windscreen and they just managed to check in on time.

1935 Monte Carlo Rally.
The most twisting road in the world. The tourist road along the coast of Southern Italy on to which we were forced by snow. There are reputed to be 5,000 bends of the type shown in the distance of 220 miles. To average 40 mph along this road entails many exciting moments. (R.H.Pelham Burn)

1935 Monte Carlo Rally.
The winter roads of Sicily. About 100 miles of unmade surface such at this imposed a severe strain on the car's springs.

Freddie Dixon wins the 1935 British Empire Trophy in which Riley's were 1st, 2nd and 3rd.

Rupert Riley gives him a well earned drink as the car pulls up.

The one and only Freddie wins again.

The winners are shown above. It's a pity that we have no pictures of the party held that evening.

Walter Handley lapped at over 110 mph in Dixon's Riley during the 1935 500 mile race and when this photograph was taken he must have been doing rather more than that speed. A wonderful effort for an unsupercharged 2 litre car.

1935 500 mile race at Brooklands. (Note that Dixon's rear tyre has just thrown it's tread)

F.Dixon in Riley (number 33) just behind a Singer at the Brooklands start line.

Peter Maclure at the wheel of a small scale Brooklands built by his father Percy Maclure. Seen here at Shelsley Walsh in the Thirties.

Reg Parnell's storage garage.
One of Freddie Dixon's famous Riley 6's.

The famous White Riley.
A racing TT 6-Cylinder Riley with a supercharged E.R.A. developed engine.

1935 Le Mans TT Sprite of Sebilleau/de la Roche.

1935 6 Cylinder Riley TT Sprite Racing Model.

1937 T.T. Reg no. AVC 20.

1938 B.R.D.C. 500 at Brooklands. Bob Gerard (4) won the 1500cc Class.

1937 T.T.
'Bob' F.R. Gerard.

Winning class at Hullingstone Speed Trials 1936.
R.C. Porter's Kestrel Special.

1938 Brooklands.
R.Harris in his Riley Sprite.

1938 R.A.C. Rally team of Riley Sprites.

The Poole speed trials 1939. R.J.W.Appleton's Riley engined special.

Production Models

1929 Riley Stelvio 14/6.

1931 Riley 14hp Alpine 6 Cylinder Tourer.

1932 Riley 9hp Gamecock.

1932 9hp Standard series engine.

1933 Riley '9' Lincock Coupé.

1933 Riley Lynx Tourer.

1933 Riley 9hp March Special.

1933 Riley '9' Kestrel saloon.

*A rear view of the
1934 Riley '9' Kestrel.*

1934 Riley '9' Imp with twin spare wheels.

1934 Riley '9' Lynx.

1934 Riley Monaco.
(Special Series)

1934 Riley Mentone 12/6.
(Publicity Photograph)

1936 Riley 12/4 Falcon.
(Publicity Photograph)

1934/35 Riley M.P.H. 2 Seater. Reputed to be the prettiest Riley ever built. (Publicity Photograph)

*1936 12/4 6-Light
Kestrel.
(Publicity Photograph)*

1935 Riley Motor Club Works Rally.

A Riley 12/4 Falcon exiting the Mersey Tunnel in Liverpool, England.

1937 Riley 18hp V8 Adelphi engine.

1936 Riley 1½ litre Kestrel. (Publicity Photograph)

1937 Riley 1½ litre Falcon.
(Publicity Photograph)

1937 Riley 1½ litre Lynx Tourer. (Publicity Photograph)

1937 Riley 1½ litre Falcon.
(Publicity Photograph)

1936 Riley 1½ litre 6-Light Kestrel. (Publicity Photograph)

1936 Riley 1½ litre Merlin.
Showing the front seats.
(Publicity Photograph)

1936 Riley 1½ litre Merlin.
Showing the battery position.
(Publicity Photograph)

1935 Riley 9hp Merlin Saloon.

Victor Riley opening the door of a 1936 Riley 9hp Merlin.

1937 Riley 1½ litre Kestrel.
(Being put to good use)

1937 Riley 1½ litre Kestrel.
(Having fun in the snow)

1937 Riley16hp Big Four Adelphi Saloon.
(Capable of over 80 mph)

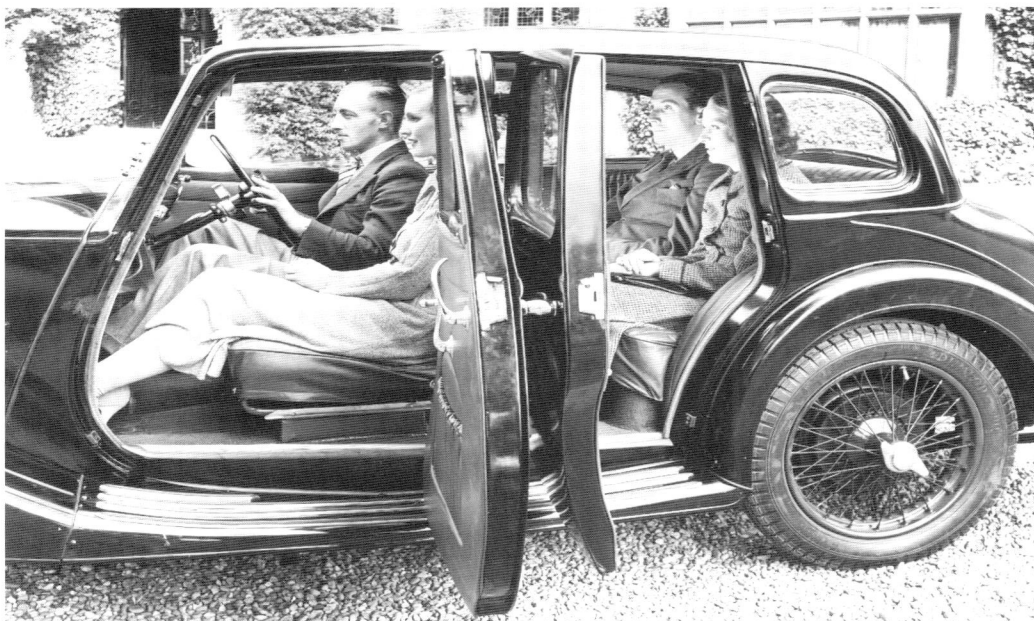

1937 Riley 9hp Monaco Saloon showing a roomy interior.
(Publicity Photograph)

1936 Riley Pre-selector gear.
(Publicity Photograph)

The Nuffield Era

Two 1946/47 Riley 1½ litre drophead coupé's.

*Portsmouth Police with
a Riley 2 ½ litre.*

Gloucester Police officers in a Riley 2½ litre RMB Patrol car.

A Gloucester Police officer showing the radio set in the boot of a Riley 2½ litre Patrol car.

A line up of Riley 2½ litre Patrol cars used by the Gloucestershire Constabulary.

The interior of the 1948 Riley 2½ litre Roadster 2/3 seater.

1948 Riley 2½ litre Sports 2/3 seater.
(When the hood was down, the wide windscreen could be folded flat on the scuttle)

1948 Riley 2½ litre Sports Roadster.
(Publicity Photograph)

An RM Engine and Gearbox.
(Publicity Photograph)

Tracking alignment on an RM.

The 1950 Rally Team.

Arriving at Monte Carlo.

Glad of a rest.

1948 Riley 2½ litre saloon. (Publicity Photograph)

1948 Riley RM shown here at Admiralty Arch in London.
(Publicity Photograph)

A Sunbeam Talbot 90 leading the Riley RM on the Monaco Grand Prix circuit at Monte Carlo 1952.

The first KLM 1 seen here in Brighton, England.

T.C.Harrison in the Riley Ulster Sprite just pulling up to the start at Prescott Hillclimb July 28th 1946.

T.C.Harrison taking the Orchard Corner at Prescott Hillclimb July 28th 1946.

J.M.Hendry 1866cc Riley MPH leaving the courtyard in the Scottish Car Club Speed Hill Climb at Boness in 1948.

J.M.Hendry at the top hairpin.

A Riley 2½ litre seen at Silverstone 1949.

Silverstone 1949.

*Silverstone 1949
entering Club corner.*

*Silverstone 1949
exiting the same corner.*

Riley within B.M.C.

Victor Leverett, Victor Riley and Lord Nuffield sharing a joke.

1955 Riley Pathfinder.

Norfolk Police Riley Pathfinder.

1962 Riley One-Point-Five.
(Publicity Photograph)

Riley Elf Mk III. (Publicity Photograph)

The Riley stand at Earls Court in 1955 showing a Pathfinder.

1963 Riley One-Point-Five Mk III.
(Publicity Photograph)

1962 Riley One-Point-Five.
(Publicity Photograph)

The Earls Court Motorshow in London.

1961 Riley Elf Mk I.
(Publicity Photograph)

1966 Riley Kestrel 1100 c.c. MkI.

An internal view of the 1966 Riley Kestrel.

1959 Riley 4 Sixty-Eight Farina Styling. (Publicity Photograph)

1966 Riley 4 Seventy-Two. (Publicity Photograph)

1966 Riley 4 Seventy-Two. (Publicity Photograph)

The facia of the new Riley One-Point-Five is in polished walnut and has a full range of instruments including revolutionary safety features. A sponge rubber protection rail above and below the facia, a dished type steering wheel and safety glass all round.

Showing the duo-tone of the seats in leather with leathercloth on the non-wearing parts. Ashtrays were fitted to each front door, also all windows were fully winding.

The diagnostic bay at the Cowley repair shop. Rolling road, wheel balancer and steering geometry check. All equally suitable for car and light van.
(Picture showing mixed B.M.C. models)

Riley/B.M.C. Competition Cars

Ian Walker driving his Riley One-Point-Five in the 11th R.A.C. British Grand Prix at Silverstone.
July 19th 1958. (Supporting race)

Riley One-Point-Five at the B.R.S.C.C. Brands Hatch meeting on Easter Monday April 7th 1958.

1961 Riley One-Point-Five cornering at speed at Church Lawford.

Montlhéry 21st Ocober 1955. A Standard Riley Pathfinder covered 108.03 miles in the hour. Officially controlled. The driver was R.C.Porter.

The Pathfinder seen here on the banking at Montlhéry.

Two images showing the Riley One-Point-Five (LRG 222) in the 1962 Monte Carlo Rally.

Taken outside the Chatéau Impney in Worcestershire, England before the start of the 24 hour Rally of 1961. L.D.Evans, P.T. Apperley, J.E.Evans and A.D.Holmes proved to be the winning team to whom the Paragon Trophy was awarded.

Riley One-Point-Five chasing an MG Magnette at Stowe corner (Silverstone) in 1958.

Last of the Glasgow starters. Les Leston and Paddy Hopkirk in their Riley One-Point-Five leave Blythswood Square on the Monte Carlo Rally in 1961.

Riley Pre-Production Models And Ones Never Produced

1939 16hp Prototype Drophead (modified before production)

Riley 12/4 Army Tourer (Lynx Derivative)
(Prototype only)

A fine example of a 1932 Riley Gamecock prototype owned by Gerard van't Hoog of Holland.

1932 Riley 9hp Falcon Saloon.
(Prototype)

Riley Brooklands four seater.
(Prototype only)

1935 Riley 1½ litre Falcon. (Prototype)

1932. Donald Healey in a Riley Gamecock (Prototype)
24 Hour Riley Motor Club Trial.